MW00389276

Unbearable Hotness

A Play in One Act

By Gabriel Davis

gabriel@alumni.cmu.edu
gabrielbdavis.com

Cast
3 w, 3 m

Characters
(In order of appearance)
Andrew
Benny (Beatrice)
Chuck
Jill
Brandon
Marisa

(Andrew and Benny, hanging out in Andrew's room. Benny is dressed like a guy, acts like a guy).

ANDREW

Dude, Marisa is so hot!

BENNY

True that.

ANDREW

I mean, she is painfully hot.

BENNY

True, true.

ANDREW

I mean, when I think about her, dude, it's like DAMN. Hot. Hot. Frickin' ahhhhhhhhhhhh. It's like burning my balls off how hot she is.

BENNY

Yeah, she looks good man.

ANDREW

She does, damn. Damn! I just want her. I have to have her.

(Enter Chuck)

CHUCK

Hey.

BENNY

Hey Chuck.

CHUCK

Hey guys, have you seen Marisa?

                    ANDREW
Why? Is she here?

                    CHUCK
That's what I heard.

                    ANDREW
Holy shit, holy shit, holy shit!

                    CHUCK
What's up with him?

                    BENNY
Something about his balls burning off.

                    ANDREW
She's here in my house?

                    CHUCK
That's what the guys doing the keg stands downstairs said.

                    ANDREW
I can't believe it worked. It actually worked!

                    CHUCK
What worked?

                    ANDREW
You throw out a net. "House Party" – "Free Beer" – "Free
Vodka" – "Free Grub." Figure you'll catch lots of guppies, a
few snapper, some sea bass, if you're lucky a blue marlin but
not – you don't expect to catch a WHITE WHALE! We have
got a White Whale on our hands, boys!

                    CHUCK
Do you know what he's talking about?

                    BENNY
Marisa.

                    CHUCK
You're saying Marisa is like a white whale?

                    ANDREW
Yes!

                    CHUCK
I don't get it.

                    BENNY
He's using fish for like, levels of hotness.

                    ANDREW
Right. The guppies are like the plain Janes, the snapper are
the cute, perky chicks, the sea bass got some curves, the blue
marlin are pretty smokin' and Marisa is, she's –

                    BENNY
Like the White Whale of hotness.

                    ANDREW
Exactly!

                    BENNY
And he wants to harpoon her with his Moby Dick.

                    ANDREW
Just call me Ishmael!

                    BENNY

No, dude, Ishmael was like the narrator guy on the periphery of all the action.

CHUCK
Ahab was the guy chasing after the White Whale.

ANDREW
Just call me Ahab!

BENNY
Now you got it *Ahab*! Up top!
        (Benny and Andrew high five)

ANDREW
The question is, now that she's so close I can almost-

BENNY
Smell the blubber?

ANDREW
How do I harpoon her?

CHUCK
By, by telling her how beautiful she is!

ANDREW
Nice!

CHUCK
By telling her you understand her at a level no one else does.

ANDREW
I don't really know her that well but ... interesting.

CHUCK

By telling her the hundreds of hours you spent together as kids were the most sacred hours of your life so far.

                    ANDREW
I didn't know her until freshman year.

                    CHUCK
That your family connection has forged an unbreakable bond betwixt you!

                    BENNY
Dude, you said "betwixt" – hah!

                    ANDREW
Yeah, I can't say any of that, Chuck.   That's totally not going to work.

                    CHUCK
Why not?

                    ANDREW
Because it's factually completely inaccurate and sounds kinda weird.

                    CHUCK
You know Ahab dies trying to get Moby Dick. Are you willing to die to get Marisa, Andy?

                    ANDREW
Uh, I don't know.

                    CHUCK
When I was a little kid, I'd swim after her in an inflate-a-pool. Now I'm grown and I'm in the ocean of adulthood. I'm still swimming, but now I don't have any water wings. I may drown. I may drown trying to love her.

BENNY

Heavy.

ANDREW

Yeah, Chuck, this is a party, man.

CHUCK

Oh, God, why can't I be with her? Why!? Why!?
(Falling to his knees)
Oh, dear, God in heaven. Please, please, please if you have
any mercy, please just let me have her. Just one light touch,
one little kiss. A smile, I'll even take just a smile. Or a look.
She hasn't looked at me in a week.
(Beat)
And last week, the only reason she looked my way is I threw
my body, like a ragdoll, onto the campus green as she walked
by. My perfect white jeans and white button up shirt grass
stained beyond bleaching. I did it for her. I'd do it again! I
was jumping to catch a Frisbee some guy had thrown to
someone else. I wanted to make it look like I was one of those
cool guys who plays Frisbee on the campus green. I had
actually been reading Proust under a nearby tree. She saw me
with the Frisbee and she was like "Nice catch Chuck."
(Beat)
"Nice catch Chuck."
(Beat)
She used to look at me all the time as children. Our mommies
would give us baths together. There we were, covered in
Johnson and Johnson baby wash, rubber ducks floating by.
Why can't it be like that anymore?
(Chuck lays on the floor and begins softly weeping)

ANDREW

Well ah ... people drift apart ... I guess.

BENNY

(To Chuck)

You are a big downer, dude. You're like a human turd of weirdness and misery.

(Enter Jill)

JILL

Hey guys.

ANDREW

Hey Jill.

BENNY

Jills! Jil-la-la-di-dah!

JILL

What's up with Chuck?

ANDREW

He's love sick.

JILL

Who with?

BENNY

Marisa.

JILL

Uch, she is such a bitch.

ANDREW

Aren't you two best friends?

JILL

Were. Past tense.

BENNY

What happened Jills?

JILL

She broke my boy Tim, Jake, John, Pete, Allen, Larry's hearts
that's what. I can't watch the carnage anymore. I'm sick of it.
Look what she did to Chuck.

CHUCK

No, no, I'll be fine. I just … need a few minutes alone. So uh,
hey Andrew, I'm just going to find a quiet corner in your
house somewhere and hang out.

ANDREW

Excuse me?

CHUCK

Don't worry, it won't be creepy.

BENNY

Dude, if you have to say "it won't be creepy" its already
frickin' creepy.

ANDREW

Whatever man, go be alone and creepy. No worries. If you
get bored, there's free beer, vodka and grub downstairs.

CHUCK

And somewhere in this house … the most wonderful thing of
all. Marisa!
        (Exits)

JILL

Another lost soul.

                            BENNY
Yeah, lost like his marbles.

                            JILL
It's not surprising. The longer they pine for her, the crazier
they seem to become.   He's known her since they were kids
so … had the most exposure, went the craziest.

                            ANDREW
Is that supposed to scare me?

                            JILL
Oh, don't tell me – not you too?

                            ANDREW
All I want is a little taste. One nibble.

                            JILL
You know how Cats love catnip.   But it makes them all crazy,
right? That's Marisa. She's like catnip but for men.

                            BENNY
She's man-nip!

                            JILL
You got it Benny. She's bad news, Andrew. Steer clear.

                            ANDREW
I don't think I can.
        (Beat)
I'm Ahab, Jill. She is my White Whale. And nothing you can
say will stop me

                            JILL
What is it about her?

ANDREW

I – I don't know. That's a great question. I mean, does she
have a pretty face? Sure. Perfect, pouty lips? Yeah. Wicked
cute smile? You bet. Soft, supple legs that go on for miles?
Most definitely. But there's something else too. Something
intangible.

JILL

Her unattainability?

ANDREW

How is it that someone could be so … ridiculously smokin'
hot … so absurdly irresistible, yet no man, no man on campus
has …

BENNY

Tapped that?

ANDREW

Have some class, Benny.
        (Beat)
But yeah, what Benny said.

JILL

Ugh, you sound just like Brandon.

BENNY

Her boyfriend.

JILL

Ex.

BENNY

Since when?

JILL

Since last night.

BENNY

What?

JILL

You know, for two years, I beg him to transfer here, so we can be together. "Oh no" he says, "some of my credits won't transfer over, I'll have to spend like an extra semester or a summer to catch up." Then on his visit over winter break I introduce him to Marisa.
    (Beat)
Suddenly, he changes his tune. "What's one summer when I can be near you?" And he transferred.

BENNY

But you were thrilled…

JILL

For like two seconds because I thought it really was about me and I was really, really happy until every other word out of his mouth started to be …

ANDREW
(Running toward doorway to his room, waving)

Marisa! Marisa, Marisa, Marisa!

BENNY
(Singing)

"I once knew a girl named Marisa!"

ANDREW

I guess she didn't hear me. Did you guys see!? She was just outside my door on the stairwell … walking up the stairs. My stairs!

BENNY

Oooh, a Marisa sighting!

JILL

So … anyway … last night was the last straw. He was
repeating her name over and over in his sleep, "Marisa, oh,
Marisa, oh, Marisa!" I wake him up and I say, "What were
you just dreaming about?" He tries to play it all innocent
"Uh, nothing. What do you mean?" And I'm like, "it's never
going to happen." And he's all, like-

BENNY

"To dream the impossible dream! To reach the unreachable
star!"

JILL

Pretty much. I mean, at first he kept playing the innocent
card, like, "what's never going to happen?" And I'm like
"Marisa! You and Marisa!" And he's all "Why would I want
to be with Marisa!? You and I are together."
        (Beat)
And I'm like "Well what if we weren't together, would you
consider being with her?"
And he says, trying to act casual "I guess, I'd be open to it.
Why? Did she say something about me?"
        (Beat)
And I say "No! Did you not hear me when I said it's never
going to happen!?" And he's all offended, "Well, 'never' is
pretty harsh. I mean, I'm pretty good with the ladies." And
I'm like "Not from where I'm standing, buddy!" He goes, "So
are you saying you want to break up?" I go "No, you're
saying that." And he says … he says, "I can't get her out my
mind, I'm sorry, I can't help it." So I say to him: "You're
throwing our relationship away for nothing. She's like fort
knocks, nobody cracks that!"
        (Beat)

And he says, "Well, not without the key. But you can help me. Please, if you ever loved me, please tell me the secret!"

ANDREW

What secret? What secret?

BENNY

Dude, everyone knows there is some movie star Marisa adores. If a guy can really make her believe he sees that movie star in her ... well it's like the key to her ...

JILL

Heart. Keep it classy Benny.

BENNY

Right. But she won't tell who the movie star is... it's a secret.

ANDREW

(to Benny)
How are you just telling me this now?
(to Jill)
Is it true?

JILL

It's like an urban legend.

ANDREW

What does Marisa say about it?

JILL

She claims it's true, but-

ANDREW

Who is it then? The movie star?

JILL

She didn't tell me.

ANDREW

You're her best friend-

JILL

Ex best friend!

ÁNDREW

You must have an idea...

JILL

If I knew I would sell it to the highest bidder.

ANDREW

Ok, what are her favorite movies?

OFFSTAGE MALE VOICE (OMV)

Hey! What the fuck Chuck! Come back here! OH FUCK, CHUCK!! I'm going to kill you!

ANDREW

Ugh. I'd better go see what's going on.
(Beat)
To be continued!
(Exits)

BENNY

There's something you're not saying, Jilly-bean.

JILL

Honestly, I have no clue what movie star she adores. If there even IS one.

BENNY

It's something else.

JILL

Why do you say that?

BENNY

How long have we known each other?   Just going to leave old Benny in the dark?

JILL

Please.

BENNY

You dump your boyfriend for being a prick, sure … makes sense, I fully support it. Hell, he was a dick before any of this Marisa stuff happened.

JILL

True.

BENNY

Yeah, I'm proud of you on that front. Good move.

JILL

Thanks.

BENNY

It's ditching Marisa as your best friend.   That's what I can't understand.

JILL

Shouldn't this make you happy?

BENNY

I'm good with *second* best friend.

JILL

Ha, ha.

                    BENNY
No really, I know some girls would dump their best friend
over some stupid guy. But you're not some girls. He wasn't
worth it, and even if he was … she didn't actually DO
anything.

                    JILL
You've got to swear to keep this quiet, Benny.

                    BENNY
Lips are sealed.

                    JILL
Marisa is gay.

                    BENNY
Get out.

                    JILL
She's gay, but she won't tell anyone. I'm the only person
she's told. And after she told me, she … tried to kiss me.
Well she did kiss me.

                    BENNY
Was there tongue?

                    JILL
Benny!
        (beat)
Yeah. There was.

                    BENNY
And?

JILL

And I didn't totally hate it.

BENNY

Really?!

JILL

So after ... Marisa says, she says she's scared to come out by
herself ... but she thinks she could do it if I would come out
with her.

BENNY

What did you say!?

JILL

What could I say? Just because I felt a little chemistry doesn't
mean, it doesn't mean I'm gay. I mean, one kiss with Marisa
and it's not like, I mean I'm still attracted to boys – even
though most of them are idiots – I still ...

BENNY

(Italian accent)
Like-ah de penis?

JILL

Something like that.   I can't just switch sides on a whim.
And that 's when she says, "So don't do it on a whim. Do it
after we make love."

BENNY

What did you do?

JILL

I did her.

BENNY

Awesome! Really!?

JILL

No, not really!! But that's what you wanted me to say, right?

BENNY

Yeah …

JILL

See, this is why you're my *second* best friend. No. In
actuality I freaked out. I ran the hell out of there.
    (Beat)
Next day she shows up at my dorm. Pissed. She says, it was
really hard coming out to me the way she did. And my
"treating her like a leper" has just made it even harder for her
to ever come out.
    (Beat)
And you know what. I'm pissed. Because it's not fair, her
putting all this on me. And in fact, it's not fair that she's
staying in the closet when she has all these boys pining after
her and going crazy trying to be with her, when she could just
let them all off the hook if she'd come out.

BENNY

Yeah, and considering one of those boys was your boyfriend ..

JILL

Exactly! And what's really messed up. She admits to me,
part of why it's so hard for her, it's not the fear of how people
will see her. It's the loss of all those crazy, obsessed guys
who've always followed her around through life. She enjoys
the attention.
    (Beat)
So I say, "I bet … I bet the whole movie star thing … it's just a
game you play with the boys to give them hope. To string
them along. I bet there is no movie star. "

(Beat)
And she says, she asks if I'm calling her a liar.
(Beat)
And I say, I say – "no, I'm calling you a dyke."

                    BENNY
Oh Jill.

                    JILL
I know, I'm horrible. And she says to me, she says, "Thank
you, thank you for helping me see what it would be like if I
really came out to everyone." She says to me, "thanks to you
I'll just stay in the closet forever and let Brandon fuck me."

                    BENNY
Oh God.

                    JILL
Yeah. It's a mess.

     [Enter Brandon]

                    BRANDON
Oh crap, crap, crap.

                    BENNY
Hey Brandon!   The man of the hour.

                    BRANDON
Huh?
     (Beat)
Jill, can I talk to you for a minute.

                    JILL
Ok …

BRANDON

Alone?

BENNY

Whatever you have to say, you can say it with me here, man.

JILL

Did you just get here?

BRANDON

No, no – I've been here.

JILL

'Cause I didn't see you when I came in.

BRANDON

I was on the roof.

JILL

What were you doing on the-

BRANDON

With Marisa.
    (Beat)
But something happened.   She's – she came back down.
Have you seen her?

BENNY

We haven't seen her dude. Well … I guess Andrew saw her.

BRANDON

I need to explain to her – it wasn't my fault.

JILL

What wasn't your fault?

(Enter Andrew)

ANDREW

Hey guys. Hey Brandon.   I didn't realize you were here.
        (Beat)
Have you guys seen Chuck?

BENNY

I thought he was downstairs.

ANDREW

I'm one step closer to cracking the Marisa code here, but I
need to find Chuck!
        (Beat)
One of the guys downstairs used to work in a video store in
Marisa's hometown growing up.   Before he quit, he printed
the entire list of Movies she ever rented out. He was waving
the printout around like taunting the other guys with it. As
the guys tell it, Chuck flew in like a ninja, snatched the list out
of this guy's hand and flew out.

BENNY

Thus the yelling.

ANDREW

Yup. I've been looking all over my house, but can't find
Chuck anywhere.

BRANDON

I …. I just was with him.

ANDREW

When?

BRANDON

A minute ago.

ANDREW

Where?

BRANDON

Up on the roof.   I didn't mean to …

ANDREW

You were up on the roof?

BENNY

With Marisa apparently.

BRANDON

(Pacing)
Ok … ah … ok.
(Beat)
I just fuckin' killed Chuck. I think. I mean, he's just laying out
there. He's not moving. I don't think he's breathing.
(Beat)
I mean, there I was just up on the roof with Marissa – talking,
laughing, having a great time. I tell her she reminds me of
Sandra Bullock. I tell her I loved "Hope Floats." Who knew
those would be the magic words? Next thing I know her
clothes are off and we're loosening roof shingles like there's
no tomorrow. And then there's biting and kissing and
touching and suddenly someone starts beating on me, I mean,
just pounding on me and growling. Yeah, growling. And I
look up and there's Chuck. And I'm like, "What's the
problem?" and he says "The problem is, dude, you're fucking
my girlfriend."
(Beat)

So I look at Marissa and I'm like "You're someone's girlfriend?" And she says "No." Then it comes out Chuck just wishes she's his girlfriend but actually she's his cousin or something, so he's got these feelings of guilt about wanting her...and then he starts crying.

(Beat)

So that ruined the mood. Marissa puts her clothes on, and she goes back down through the window, back into the party. And I'm left with Chuck. Blubbering, whining, crying Chuck.

(Beat)

And he starts in on how he's just this total fuck up and maybe he should just throw himself off the roof. And for a split second I'm thinking "YES! Throw yourself off the roof! Do it!" But I don't say that. I say I "You're gonna get a girl, buddy, just maybe not your cousin, huh?" And then I give him a friendly pat on the back. A nice manly slap on the back. And he looked heavy, I mean, who knew he'd go flying.

(Beat)

Who knew he'd go flying right off the roof?

(Beat. Everyone takes this in.)

ANDREW

So … let me get this straight. You're saying that you … had sex with Marisa?!

JILL

Wow, we just broke up yesterday. Classy Brandon.

BENNY

Guys, he ALSO just said Chuck's dead.

ANDREW

How did you know she loved Sandra Bullock?

BRANDON

I didn't, I just genuinely liked *Hope Floats*.

                    BENNY
I wouldn't admit that publically.

                    ANDREW
Wow, that's amazing.

                    BRANDON
It was.

                    ANDREW
What are the chances?   Sandra Bullock!

                    BRANDON
Yeah, I couldn't believe my luck.

                    ANDREW
Was kissing her like tasting a rainbow?

                    BRANDON
Kind of.

                    JILL
And what was kissing me like?

                    BENNY
CHUCK DEAD!

                    ANDREW
Yes, yes. Alright, alright.
        (Beat)
The poor bastard.
        (Beat)
Which side of my house did you push him off of?

                         BRANDON
I didn't push him.

                          BENNY
We should call the police.

                         BRANDON
That side.
        (Beat)
I didn't mean to…

                           JILL
Was she was worth it?

        (Andrew walks to window. Opens it.)

                         ANDREW
Chuck?! Chuck!? If you're alive, twitch something!

        (Jill leans out window too).

                           JILL
Oh crap, he's not twitching.

        (Brandon leans out window)

                         BRANDON
No twitching, no twitching at all god damn it!

                          BENNY
Great! No twitching! Maybe we should call 911 now?

        (Enter Marisa)

                         MARISA
What's going on outside? What's everyone looking at?

(They turn to look at her)

EVERYONE (EXCEPT JILL)
(Don't have them all say her name simultaneously ; -)
Marisa!!!!!

MARISA
Hey guys.

(Brandon quickly moves to her and takes her hand)

BRANDON
Marisa, I've got some bad news. Here, sit down. I don't want
to *Blind Side* you with this information.

JILL
Did you seriously just say *"Blind Side"*?

MARISA
(Giggling at Brandon, maybe touching flirtatiously)
Oh, I love that movie. *Hope Floats* and now *Blind Side*. You're
on a role tonight Brandon.

JILL
Really Marisa?

BRANDON
I'm sorry about what happened up there.

MARISA
It wasn't your fault. He's always moping around me like that.
I just couldn't stay up there and watch another meltdown.
(Beat)
Do you know if he's still up there?

BRANDON

No, he … came down off the roof.

MARISA

Oh, good. You helped him down?

BRANDON

Um … I wouldn't say "helped" …

MARISA

Well, I know it's probably upsetting to see him like that but …
don't worry, he's always bounced back before. Don't see why
this time would be any different.
      (Beat)
You're a good guy to stay up there with him.

(Andrew moves in to sit on other side of Marisa)

ANDREW

Hi Marisa. It's me Andrew.

MARISA

Oh … Hi.

ANDREW

We had "Classics of American Literature" together freshman
year? Remember, one time after class, I went up to you and
said, "Call me Ishmael"?
      (Beat)
Well … I just wanted you to know. I'm sorry about that. I've
matured since then. You can call me "Captain Ahab" now.
      (Beat)
Also, this is my house. I'm the guy hosting this party.
      (Beat)
Thanks for coming.

MARISA

Oh, sure.   Great party.

ANDREW

Yeah …. listen, we have some news to share with you.   It's
going to be heavy.   It has a lot of *Gravity*.
       (Beat, no response from Marisa)
Gravity.
       (Beat)
Like the movie with Sandra Bullock.
       (Beat)
Who you also remind me of.

       (Marisa just looks at him a moment)

MARISA

Oh. Thanks!
       (Half hearted)
Yeah, Gravity was sooooo good.

JILL

Please. Like you even care about Sandra Bullock.

MARISA

I really do. She's my idol.

ANDREW

Listen, Marisa …

MARISA

Yes?

ANDREW

Chuck is … Chuck has … well Chuck's dead.

MARISA

Excuse me?

                    ANDREW
Brandon killed him.

                    BRANDON
It was an accident.   I just gave him a light tap on the back.

                    JILL
You mean a manly shove?

                    BENNY
Andrew your house is a dead zone.
        (Beat)
Sorry. No pun intended. I can't get any bars in here.

                    JILL
Wow Benny. Is now really the time to worry about your cell
reception?

                    BENNY
Yes, yes – now IS the time.   Because we need to call the police
and report a murder!

                    BRANDON
Stop saying that. It wasn't a murder.

                    ANDREW
Well … you might say it was a *Murder by the Numbers*. Right
Marisa?

                    MARISA
Are you going to just keep working Sandra Bullock movies
into your sentences?

                    ANDREW

Depends. Do you like it?

                    MARISA
I'm having a little trouble understanding what is going on.
Chuck is .. what happened to my cousin?

                    BRANDON
I mean, he might have thrown himself off for all I know.
Maybe at the same moment when I went to pat his back, he
jumped. I mean, that would explain it far better.

                    ANDREW
Or maybe it was just *A Time to Kill.*

                    JILL
Really, Andrew, give it a rest.

            (Trying to get cell reception, Benny has climbed to
            some very high, awkward spot in the room. Maybe on
            top of a couch or a table)

                    BENNY
One bar.   Right …. here I get one bar.

                    ANDREW
Yep, I make all my calls from there.

                    BENNY
Lost it.

                    ANDREW
Yup, that happens.

                    MARISA
I'd like to see him.

                    BRANDON
He's just laying out there.

                    MARISA
Where?

                    BRANDON
Out the window.

         (Marisa goes to the window and looks out)

                    BENNY
Got it again!

                    ANDREW
Alright!

                    BENNY
Ok 9 – 1 – 1.

                    MARISA
Where is he?

                    BRANDON
He's right there.

                    MARISA
Where?

                    BRANDON
On the lawn.

                    MARISA
I don't see him.

         (Brandon leans out window. Pause.)

BRANDON

He was just there.

BENNY

Hello, I'd like to report a –

(Enter Chuck, disheveled, covered in dirt, grass and a bit scraped up)

EVERYONE (EXCEPT BENNY)

Chuck!!!!

BENNY

No, I didn't say I would like to report a Chuck. I said I would like to report a …
            (Realizing Chuck is in the room)
Um … sorry, false alarm.
            (Hangs up)

CHUCK

Marisa!

MARISA

Chuck! You had me so worried.

CHUCK

Marisa.

MARISA

Here, come sit down.
            (to Andrew)
Can you get up?

ANDREW

Oh sure. Sure. Yeah, Chuck man. Sit down.

                    CHUCK
Marisa.

                    MARISA
You've had a terrible fall?

          (Hugging himself to her)

                    CHUCK
Marisa, Marisa, Marisa.

          (Patting him on the back)

                    MARISA
There, there, Chuck. There, there.

                    CHUCK
Marisa….Oh … Marisa.

                    BRANDON
For a second there, you had us pretty worried, Buddy.

                    JILL
We were about to see this guy go away for Murder One.

                    ANDREW
Technically, Chuck could probably still press charges.

                    BRANDON
I didn't do anything, tell them Chuck!

                    CHUCK
Maaarriiiisssssssaaaaahhhhhhh.
          (Breathing her in)
Mmmmmmmmmmmm.

MARISA

You've been through quite an ordeal.

CHUCK

I have. I have.

BENNY

You took quite a fall, how are you feeling guy?
        (Beat)
Sorry about calling you, and I quote "a human turd of
weirdness and misery."

MARISA

Chuck how are you?

CHUCK

Better now. That I'm here. Where I belong. In your arms.

MARISA

Sure … but are you alright?

CHUCK

Alright? I'm in heaven!

MARISA

I mean physically.

CHUCK

I can still perform if that's what you mean.

MARISA

It isn't.
        (Beat, pulling away a little)
So … I'm glad you're not dead.

CHUCK

Never felt more alive!

MARISA
(Pulling fully away and getting up)
Ok, well ... that's good. I'm just going to...um... Boy, what a
night. I'm tuckered out, I'm just going to ... go.

EVERYONE (EXCEPT BENNY AND JILL)
Wait, Marisa! Don't go! Stay a bit. There's more beer
downstairs! The night is young.

MARISA

I really have to go.

BRANDON

But what about what we shared? Don't you think we should
... maybe continue where we left off?

ANDREW

You tried to kill her cousin, dude. Marisa, why don't you let
me give you the grand tour of my abode?

MARISA

I think I've seen most of the rooms.

JILL

And the roof.

MARISA

Right. Anyway ...
(Beat, looking right at Jill)
I know where I'm not wanted.
(Turns and starts to go)

JILL

Wait.

(Marisa stops)

That's not true ... you just ... caught me off guard today and ... the other day.

MARISA

Look, I get that you're mad but-

JILL

About Brandon ... yeah, I am ... but ...

MARISA

But what?

JILL

I have something I want to tell you.

MARISA

What?

JILL

Listen, Marisa...I'm - I have to - I know I've been a bitch to you since I found out about your – about - I think it's okay – My minds changed. Being gay's okay.

ANDREW

What did she say?

BRANDON

What's she talking about?

JILL

In fact your choice is… Well… this is all Brandon's fault. I had this dream last night. This awful horrible…a vision, it was more of a vision. At least that's what I thought last night. I woke up in a cold sweat thinking about Brandon. I knew I had to break it off … and nothing to do with the annoying fact that he's obsessed with you… honestly nothing at all.

                        MARISA
Really?

                        JILL
No, it's … what he wants - I can't be what he wants. I can't.

                        MARISA
But you said … you told me you hated me because … he was obsessed with me.

                        JILL
The truth is … he's obsessed with anyone who ISN'T me.
        (Beat)
He wants me to cut my hair, to lose ten pounds. Last night, we're making love - first off, he calls it "rumping" - we're - after we're through - he's always so sweet after - playing with my - running his hand down my stomach. But last night he grabs a love handle and says "that's super meaty".

                        BENNY
You said that to her?

                        BRANDON
Uh …

                        JILL

Now what the hell is that supposed to mean?! I mean that's a hint, right? So like I didn't know how to take that kind of - I mean who says that, "super meaty"? I'm a woman, not some Dinty More Beef Stew. So I fall asleep, don't say anything to him about it, just smile and pass out. What a wuss, right?

BRANDON

Hey, Jill – we don't have to discuss this now.

JILL

So I have this messed up dream. I'm in a fashion show, right? Brandon is a talent scout, but he's not my boyfriend in the dream. And he looks at me and says "Oh yeah girl you've got real potential." All these guys in white coats strap me to a chair and suck like thirty pounds of fat out of me through some tubes, and these little umpa lumpas are spreading it on bread, and Santa Claus is there taking it to little chil- anyway Brandon is like sculpting me. Giving all these orders, right, like "lose the upper body, enlarge the breasts, tighten up and round out the ass, fill out the legs, lose the face." So there I am. I get out of the chair and look at myself in the mirror. I'm just a pair of legs, an ass, and two humungus breasts. Brandon looks at me and says "perfect, she looks super meaty" and I'm really confused, I mean genuinely confused, I mean crap, where's my head, and I start screaming "where's my head" "what did you do with my head" "HAS ANYONE SEEN MY GODAMNED HEAD!" And I wake up screaming "Head!" so loud that Brandon thinks I'm asking him a question and he says "Sure, I'm always down for some late night head."

ANDREW

Wow dude. That's pretty low.

JILL

I mean, what is that, right?

MARISA

Jill…

JILL

And later when I ask him if he thinks, you know, if I'm
beautiful, he says; "why don't you dye your hair to look like
that chick Kate Upton, I bet you'd look real sexy." So maybe
you can understand why I'm starting to think, like, men are
pigs. Cause I mean who says that shit! None of my friends of
the non-male persuasion would say that word, "Super
Meaty". What am I a hot dog? So don't be so shocked Marisa
– I know it's been a long time in the coming. I know you
thought I was doomed to - but I'm not – don't you see – that
frickin' testosterone douchebag pig.

BRANDON

Whoa, whoa, whoa!

JILL

No, that's not fair – it's just some guys - *like Brandon* - that's
how they're - But I'm glad I figured it out. All right, I mean if
it wasn't for him – I really feel freer more alive than I've ever –
really, really, I'm not shitting you – I mean open the door, I'm
coming out! Forget men cause from now on the only thing
I'm "rumping" - NO- making love to – is, is , is…. All right I
can say it - don't wuss out now- Marisa, I want to be your
lover!!

MARISA

Oh Jill …

JILL

You said you wanted to come out together.

(They embrace and kiss)

                              BRANDON
What the hell!

                              ANDREW
What just happened?

                              CHUCK
I feel cold.

                              BENNY
I believe they just came out of the closet, guys.

                              ANDREW
Oh shit.

                              BRANDON
I don't understand.

                              CHUCK
I don't blame you.
          (Beat)
I mean, for not understanding.   I do blame you for pushing
me off the roof.

                              BRANDON
I didn't push you!

                              CHUCK
Or maybe I jumped.   It's all a little fuzzy.

                              ANDREW
This can't be happening! I'm Captain Ahab! You're my white
whale!

                              MARISA

Did he just call me a whale?

ANDREW

Like in Moby Dick! Your hotness is of epic classic literary proportions!

MARISA

A whale, really? That's what the guys are calling me now? Have I put on weight?

JILL

No, you look beautiful baby.

BRANDON

Baby?! Two seconds ago you were straight now you're a full blown lesbian!?

JILL

You have yourself to thank.

BRANDON

Marisa, this won't stick. We both know Jill. She's impulsive.
        (Beat)
There's something real between us - you must have felt it up there on the roof under the stars. And I promise you, it'll stick. What we just shared was amazing wasn't it?

MARISA

Actually … it was amazing!

BRANDON

Yes!

MARISA

Because it helped confirm for me I am absolutely not attracted to men at all. I was on the fence and that experience up there put me right over the edge. Thank you Brandon.

                         BRANDON
But … but your kisses taste like rainbows …

                         JILL
Yes they do. Like gay pride rainbows!

                         ANDREW
I was Ahab …

                         CHUCK
I was Ahab …

                         BRANDON
I guess I was Ahab … What are we talking about here?

                         BENNY
About going down now with the ship, like Captain Ahab did, chasing a Marisa we will never catch.
        (Beat)
It's a dark day for all of us guys. Losing Marisa as an object of desire … it's a real loss to all men pining after her everywhere. And it hurts. It really hurts.

                         ANDREW
Well it hurts us, right? Not you.

                         BRANDON
Right not you.

                         CHUCK
Yeah, you're not suffering.

                         BENNY
Excuse me?

                        BRANDON
You didn't actually lose anything.

                        ANDREW
Benny, you may be "one of the guys" but –

                        BRANDON
You're not a guy.

                         BENNY
What?!

                          JILL
Benny, your full name is Bernice.

                        ANDREW
It's a little insensitive to lump yourself in with us.

                         CHUCK
You're not a man.

                        BRANDON
Yeah, since you don't have a ding dong.

                         BENNY
You think a ding dong makes you a man?   Look, I can drink
you fools under the table, bench more on weights, and BBQ
like nobody's business.

                         CHUCK
BBQ?

                         BENNY

I grill meats on my grill every weekend. I slather it with homemade sauce.

ANDREW

They allow you to grill in the dorms?

BENNY

A man grills where he wants to grill.
    (Beat)
Look, boys I need you to listen, and listen good.
    (Beat)
A man doesn't need to have all that anatomical stuff to be a man. Man-ness is about grit and maturity and toughness. I may not have a ding-dong or balls, but I've got more cojones than you lot put together.
    (Benny marches over to Marisa)
Now, let me show you sissies some *Practical Magic*.
    (Swings Marisa back and kisses her deep and long. Her leg goes up.)

MARISA

Wow, Benny!

BENNY

You can call me Bernice.

JILL

Hey!

BENNY

Sorry … just had to have a moment of glory. You guys are cute together. You two. Go! Go be happy.
    (Beat)
But hey, Marisa. If anything every changes. Look me up.

JILL

This is why you're my second best friend.

                    MARISA
So ... if she's second best ... who's your best friend?

                    JILL
I think you know.

                    MARISA
What, I'm not your girlfriend?

                    JILL
Can't we be both?

          (They exit arm in arm)

                    ANDREW
So it looks like Jill harpooned the white whale with her Moby
Dick.

                    BENNY
Looks like it.

                    CHUCK
That reference doesn't make any sense.   I feel empty.

                    BRANDON
I'm uh ... going back to my other college. There's nothing left
for me here. At least there I can finish in four years.

                    ANDREW
Well, before you go, have some grub, some vodka, some beer.
I did this all for Marisa. All the parties I've ever thrown were
in hopes she would show up.
          (Beat)

I'm like *The Great Gatspy*.

                          BENNY
I think we've had enough literary allusions for one night.

                        BRANDON
Yeah, let's just go downstairs and do a couple keg stands.

                          CHUCK
We should also probably call an ambulance.   I think several of
my ribs are broken.

        (The guys exit.)

                          FIN

54127239R00029

Made in the USA
Lexington, KY
02 August 2016